Breathing in Minneapolis

poems by

Patrick Cabello Hansel

Finishing Line Press
Georgetown, Kentucky

Breathing in Minneapolis

Copyright © 2023 by Patrick Cabello Hansel
ISBN 979-8-88838-403-9 First Edition
All rights reserved under International and Pan-American Copyright Conventions. No part of this book may be reproduced in any manner whatsoever without written permission from the publisher, except in the case of brief quotations embodied in critical articles and reviews.

Publisher: Leah Huete de Maines
Editor: Christen Kincaid
Cover Art: Patrick Cabello Hansel
Author Photo: Luisa Cabello Hansel
Cover Design: Elizabeth Maines McCleavy

Order online: www.finishinglinepress.com
also available on amazon.com

Author inquiries and mail orders:
Finishing Line Press
P. O. Box 1626
Georgetown, Kentucky 40324
U. S. A.

Table of Contents

Breathing in Minneapolis 1

I The Chastisement of Breath

Lilac Time 5
Rage 7
Requiem Lake Street Minneapolis, May 28, 2020 8
June 3, 2020 9
37th and Columbus 11
Breathing Through My Pen 12
May Day Prayer 13
One Year Anniversary, Minneapolis, May 25, 2021 14
Resting Comfortably 15
No Denouement 16
Unforgiven I Wake to a Burning City 17
Revenge of the Pseudo-Ravens, 2021 18

II A Foul Wind, Upon Us All

Lament 21
Epiphany, January 6, 2020: The Drum Roll 23
Feast of the Innocents 24
At the Care Center, Last Evening Before Lockdown 25
Shelter in Place 26
What If I Will Never See You Again 28
House Lights Come On Across the City as She Dies Alone 30
Anointing Charlie in the Time of COVID 19 32
Burning the Palms 33
An April Morning in Self Quarantine 34
The Second Spring Equinox Under Covid 35
Travelling Through the Dark 36
A Midwife for the Dead 37
Epiphany, January 6, 2021 38
Question 39

III Still Here

To A Young Woman Holding on to Her DACA 43

Mourning in America 45
He is Crossing on Christmas Eve 46
A Day Without Immigrants 47
First of Her Family at College 48
Vaya Con Dios 51
On the Kill Line 53
my husband's murder *54*
Through the Plexiglass, Dimly 55
I Don't Want You to Get Shooted 57
Jackie Tries to Hold Little Abigail in Handcuffs 59
Unknown 61
Don't Kidnap My Mom Before My First Communion 63
Salvadoran Story 65
Freedom of the Press 66
Washing Away 67
My Daughter Is 68
How to Write a Suicide Sermon 69
Hallowed Ground 70
Remembrance 71

IV For the Beauty of the Earth

The Robin Builds Her Corona Nest 75
The Swallows Return to East 28th Street 76
Our Neighbor Walks His Son to the Bus Stop, 6:34 am 77
The Midfielder Bows Down for Prayer 79
Early Junefall 80
The Blessed Breeze a Day After 95 Degrees 81
The Alley That God Walks Down 82
Bath Time for the Robins, St. Luke's Day, October 18 83
Dying Back 84
After a November Windstorm 86
First Snowfall on 18th Avenue 87
A Late Arriving Minnesota Winter 88
Love Poem 90
Emergency 92
Bird Spirit Man God 95
I Will Watch You Through the Middle of the Night 97
Finding Home 98
Breathe We Must 100

Acknowledgements 102

Dedicated to the people of Minneapolis, especially the neighborhoods of Phillips and Powderhorn, who have seen so much, suffered so much and continue to give so much hope.

BREATHING IN MINNEAPOLIS

every night,
choppers grate
the air
into fire
every few minutes
a siren
lashes flesh to the mast
of wooden ships
by the whip
by the chain
by the necks
of fallen men

We mask ourselves
to protect others
from the viral hunter
singed cloth
over humid skin
eyes seeking
heaven's burnt hand
mouths
mouthing prayers
to the hidden smoke

why would breath
have a price tag

why must flesh
be sentenced to ash

in the metal madness
in the lip tuned
to righteous sneer
in the snake
watching over all

hands are lifted up
names sung over and over

skin shook over the ground
wake children
wake ancestors
wake silence

the wind beckons

I The Chastisement of Breath

flying almost intolerably   on your own breath.

Elizabeth Bishop

LILAC TIME MINNEAPOLIS, MAY 2020

after Roy McBride

It's Lilac Time
and the Family Dollar is in fire
helium balloons and sippy cups
greeting cards two for a buck
Batman birthday napkins
and miracle floor polish
dance in the flames

It's Lilac Time
purple pink blue mauve fingers
curled into a fist
flowers laid end to end
on bloodied concrete

lilac bruise
lilac skin
the lilac spin
of blue red sirens
hurting into the night

It's Lilac Time
and a boy and a girl
sleep under their beds
to avoid the shots
mothers fathers patrol
the blocks stained with curfew

Lilacs
my favorite flower
the one I brought
each year as a gift
to sweet Mother Mary
the church filled
with girls in pastel dresses
and boys in pastel shirts
little Jesus
so proud of his mom

It's Lilac Time
tear gas shrouding the street lights
non-lethal projectiles
carving holes in protestor's eyes

knee to the neck
knee to the neck
Lilacs
Lilacs
Lilacs
Neck
Neck
Neck

it's Lilac Time
the burnt aroma
of breath scattered
like blackened snow

it's Lilac Time

step out onto your stoop
smell the flowers
wash your eyes with milk
breathe—I can't breathe—breathe

it's Lilac Time
and the blossoms
barely hold the world

RAGE

God's broken little things are children
Ojo Taiye

How far are we from heaven?
As the crow flies with one broken
wing, as the buckshot rabbit
crawls under the fence leaving
fists of fur and skin on the wire,
as the Angel Mary washes her
hands in a tub of tender milk.
Braised meats sizzle on the curb-
side iron grill; blue-eyed flies swoop
into their scent and are snapped up
by the flames. We have been asked
to walk a mile in a man's shoes,
pick up our sister and wade across
a flooded street, learn who our
neighbor really is when beaten
down and left for dead, by blood,
by titles, by rabid cops, by names
unsought and un-given, by the star-
spangled garage sale of children too
young to speak. Yet we march.
Yet we sing. Yet we stand. Yes,
the flint of our tongues spark fires
that burn through our faces so that
others may see. Yes, we have given
up more than we wish. We are but
dust. We are but wind. We wait
in grief and in hope, in tender fear
and fiercer love, in silence
and in weeping if we must,
we wait for the deaf heavens
to be torn asunder and breathe.

REQUIEM LAKE STREET, MINNEAPOLIS, MAY 28 2020

> *God's fate*
> *Is now*
> *The fate of trees, rocks, sun and moon*
>
> Yehuda Amichai

Fate took a beating last night:
Knee crushing the neck, eyes
Torn by gas, the medieval
Cackling of old wood, afire.

A tree of thick black smoke
Rises from the street, concrete
Beams its roots, all air sucked
Up into scream. An older

Mexican woman stands in front
Of her shattered glass, shaking
Her head. Bits of morning fall
From her hair like lit cigarettes.

There is no loneliness left to share.
This path, first traveled by deer
And bear, under a sibilant moon.
Then the Lakota, stitching the Great

River to the chain of Lakes. Swedes,
Norwegians, Somalis, Hmong. All
Follow the trail. This thick morning,
A Bobcat rumbles towards the char,

Sirens call to sirens across the breach,
And a helicopter pummels the rising
Sun, the vanishing moon, the stars
With their hands over their faces.

JUNE 3 2020

The sirens will sound
at one pm today,
the first time in days I will
gladly greet its shrieking
slice through the sky.
Relax, my people:
it is but a reminder that
tornados can burst
from a blue true sky,
our collective first
Wednesday paean to
the mighty powers
of water and of air.

Each day, each night
for the last untold days,
sirens shrieked by our
house, our church,
another building torched,
another human holding
"I Can't Breathe"
on a stick
about to be sprayed
with a gas outlawed
around the world
in war.

Sirens.
Sirens.

Just off the coast of Circe,
Terpsichore, Melpomene
and Calliope wriggle in
their underwater grave.
Cast down by
the cruel and clever
Odysseus, they long
for sailors to lure

with their sweet
seductive songs.

The brave and selfish
captain ordered his men
to put beeswax in their ears
and lash him tighter
and tighter to the mast,
this man, our symbol
and journey home,
outwitted the sistered beauties
of Death, but, alas,
sailed off into the sunset,
without writing down
the sweet notes of the song.

And today, just off
the Potomac,
our mighty Captain
of this plagued time
summons soldiers
to clear the waves
of people crying
rocks of justice.
Their eyes and throats
cannot stomach
the acrid miasma
and so they flee,
freeing the pathway
to the God of All,
where mighty Ahab
lifts the sword
pf the Spirit
and promises
rage
such as this earth
has never seen.

37th AND COLUMBUS, THE 6TH MONTH AFTER HIS DEATH

*Two blocks from George Floyd Square,
a field has been filled with dozens of white
"tombstones" with names of black bodies
killed by police*

A shepherd, with no collar,
fixes his eyes on me from
the opposite side of the frozen
run off pond. *Will he attack?
Will he guard?* We stand on
either edge of time stilled.
The sun breaks the huge hand
of gray clouds. Two chickadees
dart in and out of the bending
stalks. No one else walks here this
exact minute, this rupture in time.
Row after row of white slabs
hold the names of just some of
the black bodies un-mattered
by police. Breonna, Philando,
Daunte, Terrance. On a tree
stump, someone wrote a small
note to George Floyd:

You can breathe now.
You can be breath.

BREATHING THROUGH MY PEN IN MINNEAPOLIS

Bottles lit, windows raped,
graffiti spilled as couplets onto
boarded-up storefronts:

*RIP, ACAB, BLM, People live
here! Don't burn us down!*

Words like machine gun bursts:
I can't breathe!
I can't breathe!

I can't scrap enough syllables
to form a word; tongue and teeth
choke each other, fire and tear gas
erase. Can a non-lethal projectile
rhyme? Can pepper spray be
deconstructed into allusive beats?

Oh, oxygen, pound through my fingers!
Oh, ink, shower curses onto this concrete flesh!

MAY DAY PRAYER

Slow, pouring rain,
followed by
brilliant sun.
My body marries
the soft chair tucked
in the corner
of the old porch.
Tea cools.
Breaths like stars
escape my lips.
Alabanza.
A new forgiveness.
The tenderness of wind.
Let me forget
myself for this one
unknowable moment.

ONE YEAR ANNIVERSARY, MINNEAPOLIS, MAY 25 2021

They are drilling holes
the next street over,
a giant hornet buzz-sawing
concrete down for the new
5-G: a faster, more expensive
way to escape. Prejudice
pollinators. People razors.
It reminds me of the electric
clippers my barber father used
on our heads, a metallic witch
divining broken secrets I tried
to hide. *You cannot hear me
when you are shouting.*
Righteousness pulses through
the air today, signifying
everything. Power interrupts,
fistfuls of change are thrown
to the ground. Heads we lose,
tails we run. Stir the boiling
pot. Toil and bubbles. Scars
soothed with stinging nettles.

RESTING COMFORTABLY

> *A defense witness in the trial of former*
> *Officer Derek Chauvin testified that*
> *Chauvin was justified in kneeling on George Floyd's*
> *neck because Floyd was resisting, instead of*
> *obeying by "resting comfortably" while*
> *handcuffed, face down on the street*

Hands cuffed,
body blacktopped,
knee to the neck.
Obey the mouth,
stop resisting,
stop breathing.
Think of your mama,
call her. Call God
into your larynx.
Pretend to be a worm
and not the name
you were furnished with.
You are finished:
bow your head,
give up the ghost.

Rest comfortably.

NO DENOUEMENT

The verdict is read.
The verdict is heard.
Streets fill with dancing,
Food free for all.

Wire stays up.
Barricades stay put.
The thinnest of lines
Turns black into blue.

Oh, for the terrible joy of cameras.
Knee pressed to the neck.
Gun drawn for a taser.
Another and another and another.

Where falls the brother, I stand.
Where stands the sister, I wait.

UNFORGIVEN I WAKE TO A BURNING CITY

Minneapolis, May 28, 2020
after José Luís Peixoto

Unforgiven, I wake to a burning city,
and walk, tenderly, on the limbs
of ghosts. I reach Lake Street as
she scrambles to pick up scraps of her
night dress: glass, aluminum door
frames, old wood, the stares of shop
owners who've lost everything.
No one breathes in my city today,
the air burnt empty by nights of tear gas,
rubber bullets and slogans, one hundred
and fifty buildings set afire. I pick
up pieces of junk, first with my eyes
then my fingers, useless prayers that
must be done. No bells ring, because time
has been abandoned, and the child who
walks alone inside me does not know
where to find peace, or if he should.

REVENGE OF THE PSEUDO-RAVENS. 2021

A few blocks from the George Floyd
Memorial lies the brick and mortar word-store
Called Hosmer Library. The last of four
libraries Carnegie built in the city. You can
only "grab and go" these masked days,
no lingering over magazines, and only
children can use computers, for homework only.

Driving down 4th Avenue, I interrupt
a small scale murder: eleven crows feasting
on a dead cat in the middle of the road.
They pick at the carcass in a secret order:
no one goes hungry, no one is pushed out
of the circle for what they have done or not

done. This feast is for all. I am almost
upon them before they rise, eleven black
seraphs, wings slapping the low winter sun
as they scatter. Their departing leaves
a wound on the ground: red meat almost
pulsing, grey fur bereft. The grateful

crows, who mate for life, who raise offspring
not their own and can make tools to make
other tools, swiftly return to the banqueting
table as I pass, no pushing or shoving, no
chattered warnings. I walk down the street
with the two volumes of MN history I am
returning: page upon page of governors
and titans, all come from Europe, now

enshrined in the names of streets and counties
and schools across the state. The crowd
of winged diners do not complain about me
breaking up the feast. They continue their
reclamation in peace. Paw, catgut, stolen
eye will grow into their wings. Meat to meat,
flesh to flesh, a bird eater eaten in peace.

II A Foul Wind, Upon Us All

*"I hear the howl of the wind that brings,
the long dreary storm on its heavy wings."*

William C. Bryant

LAMENT

> *God is the straw within the straw.*
> *Edith Sitwell*

God is the straw within the straw.

The quota of bricks not lessened.
The lash across the slaves' backs.

God is the straw within the straw.

The family shamed to give birth with the animals.
The baby barely born laid in a feed trough.
The body hunted like a plague.

God is the grass within the grass.

The withering, the scythe,
The roaring oven,
The word that does not end.

God is the flesh within each battered flesh.

Bones ground like wheat,
Wind ripened and let loose,
A goblet of sweet and bitter wine passed around the table.

God is the stone within the stone.

Lapis angularis shattered with iron rods.
The rock struck and then struck again,
The pool stirred by the angel.

God is the water within the water.

Leviathan hung by a hook.
A coin in a carp's mouth.
Rain that refuses to wash away the blood.

God is the wood within the wood.

The seed dead and sprouting green.
Limbs sheltering birds and their songs.
A box shaped like a no.

God is the night within the night.

Moon full, stars strung like teeth,
Comet slung across the horizon,
Silence hounding silence.

God is the cry within the cry.

Nipples cracked and bleeding,
The war child's mouth rippled with sores.
The storehouse locked, horses ready to ride.

God is the question within the question.

How long?
Why me?
Where are you?

God is the pain within the pain.

God is the prayer within the prayer.

God is the doubt within the doubt.

God is the hope within the …

EPIPHANY, JANUARY 6, 2020: THE DRUM ROLL

*What the United States did yesterday
should have been done long ago.*

Donald Trump, on the killing of Qasem Soleimani

Oh, for some mystery tonight,
If mercy cannot be found, as
Rockets fly in one direction
And words in another.
Words: sharpened nosecones.
Flames: mumbled elegies.
It's after midnight, and we no longer
Tell time by the sky. We look at
Numbers: body counts, hostile
Incidents, polling data. How much
Is bluster, how much distraction,
How many limbs and clumps of
Brain tissue add up to victory?
Across the web, where all is night
And nothing is calm, calls to
Support the troops, honor the flag,
Behold our resolve. *We have met
the enemy,* said Pogo, and *he is us.*
By the waters of Babylon, three
Persian kings burn their star
Charts: they have tricked Herod,
They have returned by another
Route, they look for wisdom
In the smoke of burning letters.

FEAST OF THE INNOCENTS (Matthew 2)

Those wild babies of Bethlehem,
first steps, first words, first
taste of lamb and roasted grain
stilled by a creaking sword.

They took their time, as all hired
guns do, the pain of mothers'
faces ambrosia to their skittish loins.
They killed with diligent delight,

by the sword, by a knee to the throat,
by famine and rape and commerce,
while silvery creams and blood
oranges danced on the palace's palates.

Oh, the wrath of riches barely sated.
Oh, this sorrow served on a platter.

AT THE CARE CENTER, LAST EVENING BEFORE LOCKDOWN

Each voice carries an accent: Filipino,
Liberian, Honduran, mild to moderate
Swedish dementia. At four forty-five
on the first Wednesday, the second
floor day room hosts a party for all
birthdays in the month. Not everyone
makes it. The Russian man with
cancer plays cards with the truck
driver who's lost his legs; the unknown
COVID carrier tells the nurse's aide
the story he's heard a dozen times.
5:30: pill time. Vitals check. Jeopardy.
6:15: Gray carts with invisible horses
gallop the hallway on carpet the color
of abandoned sheds. They bring chicken
patties. Double mashed potatoes.
Jell-O in old Melmac cups, covered
with plastic wrap, lukewarm tea.
Until 8:00: Families bring flowers,
cards, a cup of real coffee. Grandchildren
sit on the bed. Clergy pray and joke.
At lights out, the night nurse taps
on her rosary. Between decades, she
whispers the name of each person
on her ward, not knowing
which may have already passed.

SHELTER IN PLACE

Where are you now,
sweet Mary J,
Stabat Mater, sword-
pierced Rose of Sharon?
Your 89 years shrunk
down to an isolated bed,
voice hushed,
eyes dimmed.

I cannot visit.
I cannot lay my hand
on your head
and speak words
as sweet and pungent
as an olive grove
that blossomed early
and now faces
a late, unforgiving frost,
the air thick with smoke
from pots of fire
the family has lit
between the trees.

There is not enough
water in our bones.
The skin of our land
has run out of breath.

I want to tell you that
the robins have come back, Mary.
The first dandelions are feeding
the first, wandering bees.
The green hidden
in winter's breast
is about to burst.

Write me a song, Mary.
Open your one blind eye

and blink a message.
You are not alone.
I am alone with you.

WHAT IF I WILL NEVER SEE YOU AGAIN?

For Mary

The last time I visited,
I drew a cross on your forehead
as you slept,

and said the words,
the old, tender words.

I had no oil,
and didn't think you'd like it
if I used spit,
like Jesus had
on the man born blind.

I licked my thumb as I left

I tasted what you were leaving

Now, the care home
and the hospital,
the two barges of your body,
are closed to all visitors.

—Your mind, your voice—
—No telephone, no sound—

So I speak your name
to the gray and cluttered sky

So I scatter prayers like outdated seeds

At bible study, you
would jump to the punch line
of Paul or Moses
long before we'd read most of the passage,
your eyes too dim to read,
but your heavenly storeroom

full of verses a hundredfold:
seed, stem, grain, flour, bread.

I stare out the window

I keep watch in the shadows

Will we ever meet again?
That is heaven's part,   *
my part to murmur
your name
upon name
upon name
up onto heaven's ears,
demanding an audience,
invoking the sweet rain.

I whisper across the divide

I reach out to you with arms too short

*from W.B. Yeats "Easter, 1916"

HOUSE LIGHTS COME ON ACROSS THE CITY AS SHE DIES ALONE

Candles and lamps, as soft as the dusk
In which they shine, fluff up a bed for
Mary to lay her ashes in. They tell her:
Sleep, sleep the tent of heaven is even
Wider than you imagined. Your eyes,
Your eyes that failed these last few months
Now see the inner worlds your heart
Has stored for decades. There is no one
Who is lost. There is water in the driest bone.

I never knew my home could be this large.
From the small Southern towns to the stars
That dip into this city every evening, just
As the birds quiet into sleep, Mamas and
Babies tuck themselves into story. Even
The dreadful news each night weaves
A blanket of distant moons. Keep a light
On for me. I will visit when you are not
Watching. You will know that I was here.

This hour between, when work and school
Ease off, and families trudge home holds
Dear the smell of onions frying, the softness
Of our speech, every twilight blessing.
Our breath is never forgotten, it passes
Through halls only the heart can trust.
Believing is the deep seeing, the
Childhood love that holds the world.

Like trees walking around, like an angel
Stirring up the waters, like clouds
That reveal as much as they hide,
So are the days we cannot count.
Flesh is not a punishment thrown upon
The earth; spirit rejoices in each seed
That erupts from the womb. There is
Waking to sleep, and there is lying down.

Sleep, Mary, sleep, the light enfolds its arm.
Shine, shine, the body welcomes earth.

ANOINTING CHARLIE IN THE TIME OF COVID 19

Double latex gloves. Face mask.
Clothes I will take off on my front
Porch and step wearily into the shower.

I have been called to bless
The living one into his death.
To pour oil squeezed from the seed

Growing out of a crack in the world's
Sidewalk of grief. I hold his hand.
I pour wine into little paper cups,

The kind we used to get a sugar
Cube with a red splash of polio
Vaccine, the disposable chalice

That cradles earth's sorrow.
I drop the wager of God into
His thin hand. We pray

The old prayer. With no right
But that of friendship, I take
His face as a burnt offering,

His skin soft as a rubber doll,
The kind you chew on in your crib.
I thumb the oil over his brow, speak

These old words, these bruised names
of God. All. Forgiven.. The air in
the room hums in an unknown tongue.

BURNING THE PALMS, 2020

One palm shows a bit of green,
as if it did not know how to die.
The rest crackle as we break them
into pieces into the foil-lined pot.
It is always windy the day before
Ash Wednesday, as if the spirit
cannot abide calm before it is
commanded to be still, repent of
its waywardness, settle into the flesh
which must return to dust.
We light a match, we touch
it to the severed fronds. The fire leaps
into the air, devouring the quick
and the dead, then settles into embers
that glow red before the whole
bouquet crumbles into black.
Some years we forgot to bring gloves
and the pot burned our palms. Some
years we used snow to keep the ashes
from flying. There have been so many
deaths, so many immolations. Black
lives matter. Black ashes simmer.
Children burned alive. Families
deported in half. Hospitals bombed.
The wind stirs the pot. The smoke
on our fingers never goes away.

AN APRIL MORNING IN SELF QUARANTINE

A torrent of indescribable pleasure
Gertrude the Great, 13th century

A pair of downy
woodpeckers, dance
up the budding ash

Two fat rabbits
nibble new grass

Peach blossoms, bumblebees, the fomenting dew

This one heart
broken
open, a door
to the new
day
starting over
the blind, the lame, the dove

Wind hovers
over the wide expanse
of unseeing waters

Breathe in
bones

Hold

Breathe out
skin

Wonder

THE SECOND SPRING EQUINOX UNDER COVID

So memory will hallow all
We've known, but know no more.

Abraham Lincoln

Given a new name each
morning, the earth does not
speak it until it has heard the songs
of all its dear creatures: fox,
moose, flower, crane, moss.

Come evening, come night,
with the day's light passing,
there is still time to listen:
bat wing, owl call,
the first true wind.

Each day the sun rises
earlier, sets later; the moon
hides and peeks out,
the stars take note of the dark,
knowledge departs, love remains.

For one still moment before
the dawn, earth reveals her
blessing, then silent, waits,
for the new mercy revealed:
holy because touched,
touched because holy.

TRAVELLING THROUGH THE DARK

The doe leaps across the road.

The fawn follows.

I slow down.

The two hover in the far ditch

For that smallest moment,

The one between decision made

And action begun, the split

Second that decides who lives

And who kills. The mother leaps

Back across the road to safety,

The fawn and my front end

Coincide in space the way

We could never do in spirit.

All is silent on the night road

To home. My headlights

Enlighten the corpse

As if in anointing. A child

King slain before his reign,

A prophet no monument will note.

Steam rises from the hood like incense.

A MIDWIFE FOR THE DEAD

The first handful of dirt
is thrown in the sign of
the cross: ashes to ashes,
dust to dust. The family
follows with their offer:
a single fistful of dirt or
lone flower, sometimes all
the clay a shovel can hold.
These are the gifts for the
faithfully departed; no food
or drink for the journey, no
terra cotta soldiers, not
a single coin, walking stick
or book of incantations.
Can a pine box be fashioned
into a song? Will the concrete
vault keep time? I've baptized
more than I've buried, yet
the same verses are said,
the same, simple promise
given: this way life lies,
comingled with the deep
darkness. Grass grows
greener for a season
on a new grave. The old
trees keep the watch.

EPIPHANY: JANUARY 6, 2021

The first Wednesday sirens call
The citizens to prayer. Tornado,
Nuclear attack, civil disturbance?
A trinity of calamities to break open
The white gray world. In the shadows
Of the capital, Proud Boys brandish
Herod's toys: flags of crossed teeth,
Hot iron, bear spray; all are innocents
With the right to be afraid. Yet,
In the state of Georgia, that land of
Sweet peaches, the cry of fraud
Is washed away by the hands
Of those who mark ballots in hope;
And if only in our dreams,
In some faraway land East
Of Bethlehem camels are stirring,
Starlight beckons, and the wise
Carry inalienable gifts:
Peace, sacrifice, the wisdom
To return by another route.

QUESTION

This fever, this plague:
on the day it finally shrinks
its mad agility and slink off
into latency: will it turn
to look at the wide waters
of its death strewn
across the world,
and smile, and sigh,
and nod its head
for a job well done;
or will it lick its lips,
and inhale the scent
of havoc and heartache,
something to hold onto,
something to dream of
in its short and fitful sleep?

III Still Here

Trataron de enterrarnos, pero no sabían que éramos semillas
(They tried to bury us; they didn't know we were seeds)

Central American Proverb

TO A YOUNG WOMAN HOLDING ONTO HER DACA, January 19, 2017

I thought of you
this morning after church,
your long brown hair now
cut short, your smile
a bit more knowing.
Your dream is now deferred,
not into something like skin,
with scratches and bumps
yet shining and fierce;
but rather into the hands of
a juggler who cannot see past
the words he twirls, a man who
can only bless with his nails.

You were standing
with your mom on this corner
ten years ago, a new
arrival, eager to learn
this complicated tongue,
sharp in your school uniform,
proud of "Hello Kitty" on
your backpack. You got
all A's, volunteered at
the school and park,
kept yourself clean without
becoming brittle, wrote down
secret words that flitted
over distant flower tops.

Today, a day before the new
realm is stamped on butter
and concrete, and each sentence
begins with a dollar sign, I see
your face through the miles,
and I wonder, are you smiling?
Can you force your cheeks up
enough to show the people

you love that you will not give up?
Can you stand this long wind
without an answer?

MOURNING IN AMERICA

B will ride the bus to school today,
backpack on her lap, ear buds humming
with Daddy Yankee and Luis Fonsi.
She will explore particle theory,
themes of loss and duty in Shakespeare
and Garcia Marquez, the effects of
wage and price controls in post
war America. At lunch, she will
laugh at stupid jokes, check Snap
Chat and Face Book, text a friend
from her summer course at a well
known college. After the final bell,
she will ride the bus home, have
a snack, walk to her little brother's
bus stop, watch You Tubers, start
on homework, wait for her parents
and dinner, more homework, her
favorite TV show on Netflix, bed.
Somewhere in there—though
Google and Amazon and Apple
decry it, oppose it, the President
of these United States will act
on her fate, though he does not
know her, or know any path to gain
that knowledge. Whatever he says,
it will be about greatness, but
B and the 800,000 will know
it is about the hunt. After she
brushes her teeth and slips
into bed, perhaps she will
hum the song as she hugs
her pillow, her college, her life:
Despacito. Despacito.

HE IS CROSSING ON CHRISTMAS EVE

For D, crossing the Rio Grande

He is crossing from there to here.
No light, no angel choir,
No stolid wise men bearing gifts.

He is crossing in the solstice of forgetting.
He is crossing underneath the carriage
Of an 18-wheeler hauling burnt corn.

He is crossing the lips of those who curse,
Of those who make the cross, night after night,
Of those who cross freely, year after year.

Of those who hunt, there are none lacking.
Of those who buy, the world is without end.
Of the little ones waiting at home, a star is not enough.

He is crossing from alone to now,
From restless sleep to the dawning sun,
From humble inn to dreadful night.

He is crossing alone and with eyes.
He is crossing to take his place in the shadows.
He is crossing as the clock strikes twelve.

He is crossing before the cock crows twice.

A DAY WITHOUT IMMIGRANTS

You would not see M's
beautiful smile, or hear B's
crazy laugh. The steak would be
burned because D had not
cooked that day, the flowers
would wilt and the tomatoes
wither, since L had not risen
early to water. The boxes
would not by packed by T,
nor the parts assembled by J.
The penne with marinara
and the chicken almond ding
and the filet mignon would not
be served by A, M & B, nor
the floors mopped by R.

Your sod would not be cut
and your roofs nailed on
without A through H;
the diapers of our elders not
changed by I through P;
and the mouths of our
toddlers would not be fed
by Q through Z. And yes,
the altar cloths would stay
stained and dusty because A
had not washed, ironed and
lovingly laid them on the wood
as a nest for the body,
the blood and the word.

Yes, they all have voices.
Yes, they all have names.
I will not write them here,
citizens. Some of you have
ears connected to the heart,
but some of you have ears
connected to the whip.
Who will listen to whom?

FIRST OF HER FAMILY AT COLLEGE

When they ask me
where I am from,
I say, "Minnesota".
When they ask me
where I am really from,
I say, "Minneapolis".
(but) when they say,
"No, where are you *from?*",
I close the back of my eyes
as my mouth forms
the last letter: m
to keep from forming
the first letter: f
and drawing blood
from my bottom lip.

I am from nowhere.
I am from the rock
you broke with your
pick-axe.
I am from the time
before there was
no time.
I am from no
one I am from you
I am away
I am always away

When they ask me
how I got here,
I say, "My parents
drove me."
When they ask me
how I came to be here,
I say, "My SATs
and my GPA."
(but) when they say,
"No, how did you get *here?*",

they expect me to say
Scholarship
they expect me to say
Diversity
they expect me to say
Thank you

I am the here
that was born
between wars.
I am the here
that was mountains
before there were feet.
I am the here
where the river
runs into the forest
into the tree bark
into the veins of the leaf
into my veins.
I am the here
no one can hear.

When they ask me
what is my major,
they expect me to say
Helping
so I say
Brush fire
When they ask me
if this was my first choice,
they expect me to say
Happy
so I say
Fortune cookie
When they ask me
if they can touch my hair,
they expect me to say
Of course
so I say

Burrito
When they ask me
to sit with them at lunch
I say
Why
not

I am the lunch lady
of nuclear physics.
I am the cosmetologist
of microbiology.
I am the custodian
of 21st century cinema,
but I am not
the curator
of history,
the mirror
of culture,
the underbelly
of good intentions.

I am the daughter
Of wind dancers
I am the child
of outlaws.
I am the memory
of jungle felines.
I am the name
given to me before
your birth.
I am unpronounceable.
I am under
no illusions.

VAYA CON DIOS

Immigrants learned how to zoom in
on a funeral long before the pandemic
struck. Abuela lies in a small mountain
village of Guerrero, but her children

slaughter beef in Sioux City, clean
mansions in Wayzata, nail shingles up
and down the I-35 corridor. They cannot

return to the land of their birth for their
mother's death, for lack of a safe passage
back home, where their own citizen children,

mastering English and the rules of American
football, had talked to their grandmother on
their phones each Sunday. Death travels

in caravans and pays no entrance fees.
And each loss calls up others:
the family's avocado and mango trees,
the bodega two blocks down, chock full

of Bimbo and Coca Light, the birria and barbacoa
Mami made for holidays, the hope of one day
returning to that which is relentlessly slipping away.
Skype, Zoom, Face Time: the modern marvels

that make distance seem like closeness, that
keep connections alive—*I can see you, I can
hear you*—are a poor substitute for one short hour
of holding her hand in the garden as the sun sets.

The face you want to see, to hold and talk with,
is the one beyond stillness lying on a table
in the front room of a small house, a body that
speaks truth only the dead can bear. Yes, surely,

God has borne our griefs, and carried our sorrows,
but the grave you cannot visit ravages you with

a loneliness that reaches across borders faster
than light itself. Vaya con Dios, mami. Vaya
con Dios, abuelita. But where is God going,
and why is God's face so turned away?

ON THE KILL LINE

It was the one hog out
of twenty that didn't get
knocked out by the gas,
that came to the knife man
thrashing. All pigs squeal
their deaths, but this one,
hung by the hind legs
with an iron chain and dragged
along the relentless belt,
this hog, this one had a face
that summoned the gravest need
out of the man standing
in blood, cutting throat
after throat after throat,
it called forth the ancient hunger
encrusted in the DNA
of his gut: kill or be killed,
survive with your teeth
and hands, teeth and hands
that had not long before
been fang and claw,
remnants of a time
when this man's ancestors
had been eaten by this pig's
kind. Kindness is not a face
that death prefers. The kindest
thing the man could do for
the pig was to slash quick
and bold and deep. Blood
is no Baptism to linger under:
the next beast arrives in
seconds, his throat a paycheck,
a blessing, a curse.

my husband's murder

my husband's murder
      weapon is prayer
prayer
      for my forgiveness
prayer
      for my obedience
prayer
      that I might understand
the stress
      the power
           the burden

my husband's murder
      weapon is flowers
flowers
      after sex
flowers
      after bruising
flowers
      ripped out by their roots
and ordered
      to be replanted

my husband's murder
      weapon is time
time is money
time is wasting
time has come
      to pay the price
my husband's murder
      weapon is time

my husband's murder
      weapon is now

THROUGH THE PLEXIGLASS, DIMLY

The mouthpiece has never been sprayed
with Lysol, and the receiver retains shards
of words no mouth should utter. Remnants
of myriad biomes jump to welcome
the new microbes your skin brings.
Everything sticks: saliva, fingerprints,
promises, lies. On the first visit,
mothers, lovers, children push their hand
hard against the clouded skin, as if pure
desire, the insatiable longing to touch
the beloved behind bars could snap
the yellowed lens and bring their restless
loved one to them, body and soul. Seeing
is not believing—the fingers, the spirit need
to touch wounds, not to make them whole,
but to make them known. *I just want
to hold my baby. I just want to
bless what I cannot keep.*
                                                But no,
this window becomes this wall.
Your forearm stiffens and your biceps
ache from holding onto the phone,
but if you switch hands, your neck will
strain your face so far, that the smile
you practiced on the 90 minute bus
ride to this place, the smile that says
I'm all right, the kids are all right,
will fracture into tiny bits of glass.
Don't count the seconds you have—
this window of time is strictly
monitored. Don't convince yourself
it will soon get better. Just breathe
in the scent of the beloved
that transcends this pane that separates
the begotten from those awaiting
judgment. The plexiglass is merely
a ghost. The real eyes lie deep within.
Pretend you are a mirror.

Pretend your hand is a magnifying
glass, and your words are the sun,
focusing its love on a tender leaf.

I DON'T WANT YOU TO GET SHOOTED

*Italics from body cam video
of police shooting of Philando Castile*

four-year-old hands
around a handcuffed neck
four-year-old's words

*Mommy, be quiet.
I can keep you safe*

seven bullets
seventy three seconds
five days of deliberation
one ghostly command

do not drive a car after dark
do not be dark
do not be black

      with a license   without a license

      with a permit   without a permit

      with a record   without a record

      walking away   walking towards
      selling loosies   smoking pot
      playing in the park   being anything dark

do not cuss
do not talk
do not be who I must not let be

*They're not going to shoot me
I'm already in handcuffs*

the maximum escape velocity
of the officer's firearm times
the minimum regard for life

equals the lung capacity
of a child who
they forgot to shackle
in the back of the patrol car

how long
how long
how long
how long…

JACKIE TRIES TO HOLD LITTLE ABIGAIL IN HANDCUFFS

Jumpsuit. Paper slippers. Good Friday
wedding at the immigration jail.
Six guards in the disheveled, unused
courtroom. American flag, portrait
of the President, judicial robe thrown
over a high chair, but no judge,
no jury. Just the pastor, a wife-to-be,
the sister who helps at the restaurant,
your interpreter, a five-month
old smiling chipmunk. Handcuffs.
Leg cuffs. Do you take…to be
your wife…to have…and to hold…
—but only her hands, not her arms,
only her fingers, not her face—
till death do us part. Till the bus
with bars. Till asylum denied.
Till the flight back to China, till
the welcome of tin snipped hands,
their bars and sentences without end.

Habeus Corpus. Habeus Anima.
You have the body. You have the soul.

Then the honeyed moon: a 45 minute
family visit. Plexiglass and phone provided,
Abigail squirming and smiling. Can't
kiss the wife through the window, can't kiss
the baby, can't eat a piece of wedding cake
or tip the champagne glass into the throat
from where the deepest songs spring
forth. Just words and eyes through
the scuffed membrane that the Migra
maintains in leaky yellow. Jackie
speaks to Grace in a tongue that Abigail
may one day forget. Grace's words are
small and dipped in fish sauce. Gestures
hop on a hot wok. And in the singing

depths of Jackie's brain, each second
a pile driver slams into frozen ground.

Habeus Corpus. Non Habeus Anima.
You have my body. You cannot have my soul.

UNKNOWN

A young girl was smiling,
holding her mother's hand
as they walked away from
a beautiful night, singing
a song, skipping a little as
she looked forward to father
and brothers, but holding tight
to mother's hand, one night,
just the two of them, smiling,
singing seeds of each other
and flowers that bloom
new each day, when
the bomb tore off her
mother's arm, and her
own, and most of the
smile and all of the song
skipping in her brain,
and her mother, half
blind and full deaf
from the blast, searched
on her hands and knees
for her child, not feeling
her ghost arm with its
flap of skin flapping
in the acrid air, but looking,
calling with a voice
that could not speak
for her beloved one,
for any part of her,
her braided hair, her
dress, her new sparkly
shoes, and there was no
sound or sight of her,
no smell but the one hell
makes when laughing,
and the world rose up
and did nothing,
did not publish her

name or her school
picture, because it was
our bomb that fell,
our right proclaimed,
our night rained upon
the land we had chosen.

DON'T KIDNAP MY MOM BEFORE MY FIRST COMMUNION

for J

She crouches behind
the stove on the 4th floor
of a building with no elevator,
no front door, no smells
but rum, urine, frijoles,
flowers, fried fish,
t-shirts and pork.
She breathes as softly
as her mind will let her,
with knocking at the door.

Who could it be?
A machete?
A tiny telegram from Tio?
An angel whose face
is on backwards?
The little peephole
is a magic pipeline:
good things come in small packages
and bad things, too.

Her body is twelve, skinny
enough to squeeze behind
the stove, tight enough
to attract mustaches,
fingertips, *maldiciones*.
Her eyes are mousetraps
being nibbled.
She prays with her thumb,
her nightgown, the stuffed
bear she thought
to bring along.

She remembers
the story from First Communion —
the five thousand fed,

five little breads,
two small fish
given by a young boy.
"But it could have been you,"
the pastor said. "It could have
been your hands
holding up the miracle."

She looks at her hands,
browned like stove grease,
white knuckled, red
in the creases.
I will be bread, she thinks.
I will be a fish:
a tiburón, a shark,
something that is
difficult to catch.

SALVADORAN STORY

We sit on sacks of corn
donated by
The People of the United States,
and listen to the woman
tell how her daughter
and her daughter-in-law
were *disappeared.*
When she went to the police,
they took off her blouse,
heated their machetes
in the fire
and held the tips
under the folds
of her breasts
until they were done,
and then they sent her home.

FREEDOM OF THE PRESS

For Jamal Khashoggi

Two private jets. Fifteen men.
A bone saw. Multiple messages,
Pillowcase promises: "just" an
Interrogation gone wrong, a
Terrible act that merits no
Consequences. How much bleach.
How many bags. The same video
Played over and over: A man not
The man walking down a side street.
 A widow never married. Talks over
Sweet tea and dates. Sentences like
Breath on a cold fall day: fog, mist,
Disappearance. A coin with a hole
In the middle, clanging
On the metal sewer drain.

WASHING AWAY

He was washing his hands
at our kitchen sink, washing
and washing, the water running,
demanding more soap, this man
from Ukraine—writer, teacher,
speaker of many languages, now
reduced to one tongue even he
could not stand. A stranger in
his own mind. His wife of fifty
years leaned on the railing
of our back steps, pleading.
Each time she had passed us
on the street, she gave us a dollar
or two for our six year old's college.
Now she leaned, apologizing
for the man who barely knew her,
yelling at him that this wasn't his house.
I told him to take his time, offered
him a towel. My wife took his arm
and led him out the door and
into the late afternoon, patting
him on the shoulder and saying
"It's OK, it's OK, it's OK."

MY DAUGHTER IS

For Caster Semenya

My daughter is long and strong
She steps over mountains
She lifts sea beds with her legs
She refuses to dress in your clothes

My daughter is laughter clenched
She frees the white wind with her fist
She outruns the day
She refuses to speak as softly as a lion

My daughter is flesh of my flesh
She Titans her muscles into rivers
She prowls the earth with her bones
She refuses to inhale your words

My daughter is not your flesh, your words, your womb
She refuses to undo her body, she will not be your fear

HOW TO WRITE A SUICIDE SERMON

Get the call at night—always at night. Always from a friend of the family; a family too stunned and torn to even dial the phone. Put on your collar and dark pants. Grab the prayer book. Turn off the radio in the car as you drive. Practice useless phrases in your head until the letters start bouncing off your brain onto the steering wheel. Do not run over a child who darts out into the street. Shake hands with the dead one's family. Ask if you can use the bathroom. Eat whatever is set before you—nothing will be. Drink coffee if it's offered, even if it's late. Ask if everybody knows. Wonder why the hell you asked that. Don't ask what happened—it will come out of their mouths slowly, like smoke from beneath the woodwork of a house barely on fire. Stand up for everyone who comes into the room to bring greetings of grief. Don't judge the people who say the stupid things they always say at a death. Ask about the mother of the deceased, if the mother's not there. Ask who is coming in from out of town. Ask if you can say a prayer—knowing that they will always say yes, knowing that the only prayer on their hearts is the prayer that what has just happened has not happened. Pray for God's mercy. Drive home. Sit at your desk, not writing, not typing, stabbing the pages of the bible, asking God why mercy was missing at that one, clear moment.

HALLOWED GROUND

A lone owl calls from beyond
the cemetery gates—it is one,
it is death, it is searching.

The trees wrestle below the earth:
who shall reap the rain,
who the bones. An Angel ascends

the wrought iron fence, wings
of fire, wings of breath, craving
the flesh all mortals will slough off.

We are all hands
writing our own names

In the swale, in the low, folded
ground, babies who were born still,
soldiers who knelt rather than fight,

the hangman who hung the murderer
of the murderer of the five year old girl,
all rest. The owl calls from lone to love.

A young man drops his fire and runs.
A young woman undresses her wounds.

REMEMBRANCE

> *"...we name names*
> *that went west from here, names*
> *that rest on graves..."*
>
> *Wendell Berry*

South of town, where the creek
bends just before it enters
the river, lies a little Calvary
of my clan: grandmother, grandfather,
dad and mom, aunts and uncles,
a cousin who died before he knew his name.
I will not rest here. I will not lie.
Those beloved who follow my last
breathing will tuck me into earth
north of here, or south, deep south,
wherever my ramble and my wife
may take me. I have never taken
my shoes off on this ground, though
some late afternoons I have heard
God calling from the burning
field north of here, the corn
stubble red against the setting sun.
Today, the red tailed hawk floats
below the firmament, as twilight
gathers the eyes of all.

I shall not rest here. I shall not
hear the mist rise from the creek
nor the last leaf fall from
the pin oak yards away. But this
year and next, I will walk from
name to name, in that first breeze
of night as the sun dips below
the rim line of the good, black soil.
I will smell the earth, rising
to meet the air, a sweat offering
breath to waiting seeds.

I will let the wind carry my voice.
I will continue to call out my names.

IV For the Beauty of the Earth

Scatter in me the seeds
Of a thousand saplings.
Let grow a grassy heaven.

Yi Lei

THE ROBIN BUILDS HER CORONA NEST

It rained last night—peals
of thunder before dawn—
so fat worms should be ripe
for picking. But this mother-to-be
only looks for the best tufts of
brown grass. She plucks a
beakful, flies to the elbow joint
of the downspout where she
is building a crown for her brood.
She places the fibers in the bowl,
then butts it all down, her soft
rear welcoming each strand.
Six feet is the proscribed distance
for creatures under threat,
but there is good bedding near
my feet and so she dives to gather
what the earth is sloughing off,
then rises to add this treasure
to the new house. Soon, it will be
a cup for the sky blue eggs she
now wombs, a crown for her to wear
upside down, her soft bum a gentle
warmth to her offspring, a welcome
of new life to this quaking land.

THE SWALLOWS RETURN TO EAST 28TH STREET

Not with trumpets, or portents or exactitude,
as at San Juan Capistrano, where the winged
heralds arrive right on time for St. Joseph's
Day, two days before spring. Nor in a whirl
of wings at dusk on the soccer pitch, phantoms
skimming inches above the grass, as my long-
legged daughter sprints goalward. The swallows
do not arrive at the old church tower on East
28th Street. They *appear*. One morning, they
are there, as I walk bottles and cans to the
recycling bin; one night, as spring stretches
its tongue over the long, dying winter, and
awakes joy, they are simply there. They are
there, skirting in and out of the cornices,
the nooks where their sisters, the sparrows,
have founded a nest to lay their young. They are
there, dwelling high enough above the thawing
earth to shield their eggs and hatchlings from
raccoon and rat, yet tucked into corners where
the tower meets the arched roof, tidy avian
hermitages too small for the red-tailed hawk—
that fierce remainder of souls—to enter and
plunder. The swallows return to East 28th Street,
not by clockwork nor command. They appear,
they tarry, they praise. Their wings whisper
each summer twilight. And then, of a season,
they are gone. Not having flown away; or departed;
but simply—and unnoticed for a time—they are
absent, as fall falls slowly towards another winter
and leaves us with just a slight rift in the sky,
where all our longings for birth, for rest seek shelter.

OUR NEIGHBOR WALKS HIS SON TO THE BUS STOP, 6:24 AM

Slowly, steadily, each workday
morning, his hand on the boy's
shoulder, a boy reluctant to leave
the warm womb of kitchen, of
coloring books, of mother tending
to perennials in the early spring.
The boy passes by our house in
mourning, as I sit on the porch in
morning meditation. His little
backpack like a prison sentence
condemns his shoulders down
almost to his feet, dragging
along 18th Avenue. Today,
this day only, his father sees me,
wrapped in the Batman blanket
my daughter gave me, the prayer
shawl whose capital is Jerusalem
around my neck. We salute each
other with our foreheads.
Where does this neighbor go
after leaving his son to the wolves
of alphabet, digits and songs?
I never see him returning
by our street—to his breakfast,
to his younger son, missing
his older brother but glad for
the sole attention, to his wife
still digging—can it be
that he returns only when prayer
has trespassed into sleep, my thoughts
of God worming into the darkness
the surrounds? Or does he take
another route home? Warned
by angels in a walking dream,
he stops for coffee, for the news,
for a rendezvous with the cardinal
that has been singing for two hours,

his fire engine body glorious
against the brightening sky?

THE MIDFIELDER BOWS DOWN FOR PRAYER

It has rained three days straight,
and the Blackhawks are itching
to get back on the pitch. There's
only so much waiting that feet
can stand. I drop my daughter
and the other two girls
off at the edge of the away team's
field, and park the car under
an unknown tree. Heat has ramped
up humidity, and steam rises off
the grass like incense.
As warmups conclude, N asks
me where she can pray—it is
that hour, and each bit of earth
that is not mud is wet grass.
I am not her coach, nor
her father, but she trusts me,
perhaps because I drive her
to each practice and match,
my daughter and the others
laughing with her in the back seat.
I reply, "wherever you can,
I guess," and she removes her
jacket, lays it on the ground,
kneels on it, and bows towards
the East. Her hijab touches
the blades of grass that sparkle
with the remnant of heaven.
The ref's whistle blows
as she rises. She smiles
and nods to me, the little
cousin of a bow, and takes
the field with the other ten.
Soon their feet will dig
up pieces of earth like
buried treasure, soon the ball
will fly, soon I'll shout
"Pass the ball, N,
damn it, pass the ball!"

EARLY JUNEFALL

Hundreds upon hundreds
upon thousands, arriving
from the west, little white
spies, hovering outside
every window. I know
it's just the neighbor's
cottonwood tree, that giant
lonely beast that stands
sentinel a block away,
upwind, watching, watching
over everything. But the fluffy
botanical drones, floating on
whatever breeze fancies them,
seem more than alive to me.
A biblical plague? A mass
shedding of every pale bird
in the vicinity? Or maybe it's just
a reminder of how very few of
earth's birthed creatures survive,
and so Mother Cottonwood
needs to loose her multitudes
in such abundance the whole
sky lights up with summer snow.

THE BLESSED BREEZE A DAY AFTER 95 DEGREES

A dozen small limbs lie on our
sidewalk, the green leaves starting
to curl into their final drought.
How long do cells live when
their rivers are severed? The sky
has found the blue of its birth, and
the air around us, which yesterday was
held down by earth's iron hand,
now lifts slowly mother-ward.
In the grass, the baby rabbit relishes,
on the maple, a stark red cardinal preens,
and sitting quietly, my skin remembers
itself. This must be, perhaps this is
Eden's long lost call: knowledge
surrendered, our parents' fear shed
like scales, and the four great
rivers washing over the land.

THE ALLEY THAT GOD WALKS DOWN ON

Aluminum has fallen to a 10-year low, and so each
can of coke, each Bud Light flattened by an old truck
brings less coin to the shopping cart she wheels down
the cracked concrete. Her felt fedora tilts down and
starboard, as if scouting a giant fish hiding in the stinging
nettles and rogue raspberries ticking out behind the garage.
No Jonah today, skittering out from the swing set
trashed by the last storm. A swallowtail butterfly skins
the top of the dwarf lilacs, less fluent this year due
to the late spring. Condoms, used and unused, lie forlorn
under the bushes. A robot spaceman painted on a black
shed sings. Old tires harbor hordes of mosquitoes.
The High God of forsaken metal saunters on.

At the last house, two children play hide and seek
in an empty yard. Their mother opens the back door
and lets the Chihuahua out, and then there are three
beings scampering over the mown crabgrass and
Creeping Charlie, yipping and shouting, free as
only those fully tethered to their bodies can be.
The shopping cart stops to rest its unlubricated wheels,
and the Divine lays her arms on the crossbar. She pulls
a short leaf from her pocket and begins to chew.
Some days, her legs do not last her appointed rounds.
Some days, there is so much breath she can hardly speak.

BATH TIME FOR THE ROBINS, ST. LUKE'S DAY, OCTOBER 18

The mid-afternoon sun quivers
out from behind its clouds and
finds the shades of green
that had been sleeping
among the brown and golden fleece
of the streamside marsh. Chickadees
buzz in with their chip-chip-chip,
and on the shag bark oak the downy
woodpecker begins its search
for a tea-time feast. Blue jays
preen and snap, golden finches flit,

and in the slow bend of the stream,
one by one the robins fluff and flap
their wings in the shallows, splashing
water on their gingered breasts.
Only the males are left—their mates
have flown to Mexico and further
south—and so the pumpkin-chested
males, proud as hunters in
their vests, practice the age-old
healing proverb: after godliness,
cleanliness is best.

DYING BACK

I run the red and green push
mower over the back yard one
more time; less to cut what little
grass remains than to chop the weed
tree leaves browning up on the
Creeping Charlie and crabgrass.
Tonight, we will cover the tomatoes
and peppers in a quixotic hope of
squeezing a few more gifts from
October. Small green tomatoes hang
from withering vines. The raspberry
canes bend down, laden with almost-fruit.

In the front yard, our silver maple
and gingko hold onto their green
like visas against death, while
the fiery maples across the street
jettison their crimson fingers into
this fierce wind. It will be useless
to rake for days. Our leaves will
fly to the neighbor's, the neighbor's
to ours. Already the hostas and
sunflowers are shedding their bones,
and the flowers the bees delighted
in all summer have shrunken to seed.

All this is ordered by an ancient
call: earth and her creatures
loosing what they love to die back
into winter. Every fall, they take
the cup and drink it. Every autumn
their goodbyes ravish our eyes
with color. Maybe a tree weeps
each leaf she has held as it drops
down to rot away. I cannot know.
But there is welcome for each in
the deep dark where roots labor
among the blind beasts. It may be

that each fallen leaf, each withered
stalk dancing and dying is a tender
of incense, a prayer flag, a knee
bent to offer blessing to the world.

AFTER A NOVEMBER WINDSTORM

Leaves float downriver as if searching
for fathers, for voices, for lands unlearned;

birds that yesterday sang cornstalk and
sweet berry now dive into thickets ripe

with burr, seedpod and regret. All
the orange of the hallowed moon, all

the blood red sky of summer has been
blown from the world, leaving the char,

the gray, and the remnant green to poke
their noisy and humbled fingers at the sky.

FIRST SNOWFALL ON 18TH AVENUE

The last leaves of the Norway maple
refused to turn this fall, refused to fall
down. Now their green fingers welcome
the first flakes as fur. The ground begins,
like a dog, to sniff out this new arrival
it vaguely remembers: is it friend or
foe, rival or possible mate. Like
other years, other snows, the grass
remembers that it knows how to surrender.

The pile of leaves that Talia has not
yet bagged begin to cotton up, and
across the street, the toddler's broken
trike sports crooked white wings.
Evening slides into night, and the solar
lawn lights begin to flicker under
their silken veils. We sit with our tea,
on the porch. As the hours pass,
quiet settles over the city like a
calming womb: to drive, to shout,
to summon sirens or a gunshot
would be blasphemy. The divine
has come to breathe us down,
attended by angels who sing without
opening their mouths. This snow
will need to be manhandled tomorrow:
the car unstuck, the walks made
passable. But as we linger, and though
we shiver, the white, starlit dust of our
beginning and of our end eases us up
and towards bed. Sleep is snow's
sacred balm to the wide world.
Kiss upon kiss will fall upon us
throughout the long hours.
Let us breathe.

A LATE ARRIVING MINNESOTA WINTER

Everything has fallen, fallen, fallen.

All that is left aloft are seeds
hanging on brittle brown stalks
that once swarmed with bees;
their round heads spiked burrs
ready to leap on any beast,
and travel to strange lands
where their deaths will rejoice
in the dark, swarming soil.

Everything has fallen, fallen, fallen.

Trees are but bare bones against
a graying sky, their farthest fingers
open to receive their first winter,
as if begging, as if asking to receive
a new name, a royal inheritance
that will never die, but always fool.

Everything has fallen, fallen, fallen.

Maple, oak, linden leaves tussle
on the ground, confused by the sky
gods' caprice. Now rained upon,
now snowed under, now sparked
with a late 50 degree day. They are
shedding cell after cell, their only
memories, as they tuck their
crinkled songs into the folds of grass.

Everything has fallen, fallen, fallen.

Now, the rodents rule, squirrels
fattening on remnant seeds,
rabbits nibbling the stubborn herbs.
A pair of cardinals spy and spring
through the bushes; the next door

dog still doesn't know who I am
this eleventh year together. She
barks broken wings as I walk
out to pick the last of the sage.

All that is left to rise are seeds.

LOVE POEM

after Billy Collins
You are the cardinal's desire
singing me awake at 4 am.
You are the maple in our front yard,
waiting for the sun to run its sap.
You are the hum of the furnace,
cheery in its robust wheezing, but

I can't tell if you are
my wife or my God,
which is profoundly scary,
but also nice to know
I can ask either you
for a hug, and you will—
almost always—say yes.

I sit on the cold front porch
wrapped in a blanket and hot tea
and count the ways grey skies
change on a late winter day:
one......................................,
OK, the houses do not change
either, except for the light
in their eyes that comes on,
goes off, comes on higher up
or lower down, winking
as if to say, "I see you
and I don't mind." I can

hear you moving around upstairs,
your steps from room to room,
the way your body catches
then releases the hundred year
boards. It is like the quietest
form of thunder: no lightning,
no damaging winds, just
the bit of wonder that air
makes when it forgets itself.

The dog's slow barking
wakes my brain just enough
to know I am alive. There is
a taste of brown sugar and
silence in the back of my throat,
where words are born and
quickly fly. We are together
a far country, where distance
is an eyelash and longing a peach.
We watch for the ripening, one
glance at a time, like ravenous birds.

EMERGENCY

The blue paper gown was too large
for the little one's body, and so
it billowed into the bright air of the ER
like a welcoming sea. The nurses
had pierced the first vein they found,
swiftly and with little pain, and
the fluid in the hanging bag spilled,
drop by drop, into her whispering blood.
She sat on her mother's lap, unaware
of the great flood still waiting to flow
from the silent face above her, a face
with no desire but to have this child,
and to hold her, this morning, forever.

The little one's eyes had shuddered
but an hour before, like a stylus
mapping tremors along the fault line
of this beloved rock, floating on
on top of a restless, boiling lake,
bequeathed to us by our sun.
Her body had tightened to an iron rod
banging on the air and sounds like strange
birds dying came from her mouth and
wakened her father. He shouted for his
wife and older daughter to rise, to keep
weeping, yes, but move fast, get your
clothes on, as the overheated blood
of this child, this unknowable blessing
continued to rumble her brain, a gift
from her creator, who had anticipated
such terror even before flesh was
created, and made convulsions,
the shaking of the body by the swirling
of the brain, into a kind of noble
but frightening baptism: fire to put
out fire, a deluge of sparks to calm
the unknowable, dark depths.

The doctor counseled a spinal tap,
to rule out blood in the brain,
to give assurance to himself and
the little one's parents by piercing
the long river that carries each call
and response to every cell in every
part of the body. The parents
nodded their nervous "yes",
and held each other like worn
life vests. Mother stayed with
the blue billowed girl, as her

ten-year old sister—who had
temporarily forgotten the terror
that had thrown her out of sleep—
got incredibly bored and was
looking for something, anything to
amuse herself with. Old *Highlights
for Children* on the side table,
toys for children a bit older than her
beloved sister, but ones that no self
respecting tweener would touch;
she wrestled with her hands and feet,
until her father sat on the carpet
next to her, and started flipping
the letters on the spin-a-letter
rack, making up crazy phrases:
aardvark sinuses, and pumpkin
butts and several that ended in poop
and as they laughed and tried
to outdo each other with weird,

all the saints of Saint Christopher's
Hospital for Children on East
Allegheny Street in Philadelphia,
the nurses in their smocks colored
with cartoon characters, the orderlies
emptying trash cans and wheeling
children to X-Ray and therapy,

the line cooks in the cafeteria
deep in the bowels of the building
preparing post-surgery treats,
and even the flying giraffes
and the monkeys in tutus and
baseball caps painted on the walls,
lifted up the little one onto
their shoulders, and began
to carry her across the river.

BIRD SPIRIT MAN GOD

God fears us all
Theresa Svoboda

I woke early to beat the birds
to song. I lost. The sky shed
its darkness like skin. I sat.
Above the reach of the shagbark
maple, a royal butterfly floated,
its wings whispered wind. My voice

is bark, roughed to keep dreams
in, to keep bugs out, but today
I cannot see where I am growing.
Life, this bark of spirit we wear,
is true and not true in the same
breath—whether we sing paeans,
to the sun or dirges bent down low,

we are all held in our voices.

I will sing. I will trumpet
the name of heaven before
I surrender, I will go down
singing. There is no fear
but the one we lack a name for,
the face that stares and will not speak,
the one that walks in me each day,

and yet,

like greening leaves, like
wings, I turn to beg the sun to sing
to this earth. I am the spade,
the rake, the borrowed
glory of ancient vowels.
I have a remnant word to lift up.
Sing with me, doves and robins.
Dive into my voice

and find a worm, a seed
just right for plucking,
for flying home to bestow
upon your chirping offspring.

I WILL WATCH YOU THROUGH THE MIDDLE OF THE NIGHT

After Johanna Klink

I will watch you through the middle of the night,
the stars revolving around the sky, your fever
rising and falling, and rising again. I will check
your breathing, hold your little hand in mine,
brush the invisible dark things from your back.
I will try to comfort you. I will take note
of the dogs barking, and the old woman
rummaging the neighbor's trash
at 3:00 am, looking for cans to sell. I will walk
the hallway outside your room, and whisper
to the walls that lean in there. I will be alone
for you, I will tell you how you will feel better soon,
I will tell God why we chose your name,
and plead his mercy. I will repent
for the sins you have not yet committed.
I will watch you through the middle of the night,
when no one and no thing is calling, I will
kneel by your breathing and your eyes.
I will watch for the dawn, scratch for it, sing it
as fierce as I am able, my little voice like wings
beating against the fullness of redemption.

FINDING HOME

Let us take the last road
into town, the one
that dips ever so slightly
before it crosses the township line.

See the first yellow leaf
on the honey locust,
the one that bends
into the west wind, like wishing?

If we arrive just before dusk,
we can see the last glint of gold
off the grain elevator's roof,
we can smell the cut hay

releasing the late August heat,
and feel the swift wind
that follows the swallow's
race through the air.

There it is!—the path
we walked behind the depot
where we spooked pheasants
and pretended to pump our imaginary guns.

The broken ties on the abandoned
spur still push back on our boots
as if they recall the feel
of our footsteps on the wood

the first time we said goodbye
to this land, and the generations
it bears down on us. Remember
our feet, how they pulled

the whole of our bodies
into the earth, as if
surrender, as if hope?

Remember how we spit

out our names like nails
and shook dust from our feet?
That dirt has not abandoned.
It waits by the bend in the river,

it holds a supper pail,
and a long, slow song.
There is water there,
and there is silence.

Let us walk on, brother.

BREATHE WE MUST

I can't breathe
I can't breathe

What other three words
spark such terror?

The novel virus scars
the alveoli of the old
and the torn

The knee crushes
the windpipe
of a prostrate man

The smoke of looted
candy bars and motor oil
pummels a disposable neighborhood

I can't breathe
I can't breathe

Take out the last "e"
and the verb vanishes
into the air

Take out a man
and the city spasms
into fiery dark

Take out a loan
buy your family's first store
and watch it explode it flames

Take out a grandfather
on a stretcher, a lover, a child
and never see them

again

I can't breathe
we can't breathe
breathe we must

breath we will be

ACKNOWLEDGEMENTS

These poems were born in the struggle and beauty of the lives of people in Minneapolis and beyond during the tumultuous years of 2020-2022. It is their courage, their resilience and their hope that I wish to thank most of all.

I also want to thank those poets and writers who have helped me grow as a writer, including Phillip Schulz, Jude Nutter, Ed Bok Lee, Richard Terrill, Tim Nolan, Bart Galle, Donna Isaac, Sheila O'Connor, Joyce Sutphen and Walter Cannon, the members of the third Thursday and first Saturday poetry workshops, my fiction group zoomers, and the wonderful youth poets and artists with whom I work.

"Lilac Time" was published in *Water-Stone Review*

"Breathing in Minneapolis" was published in *Nine Cloud Journal*

"Rage" was published in *Snapdragon*

"Requiem Lake Street Minneapolis, May 28, 2020" was published in *Black Sunflowers' Anthology HOT*

"An April Morning in Self Quarantine" and "Unforgiven, I Wake to a Burning City" were published in *North Dakota Quarterly*

"Shelter in Place" was published in *Barstow & Grand*

"Burning the Palms" was published in *A Given Grace Anthology*

"Mourning in America", "A Day Without Immigrants" and "The Midfielder Bows Down for Prayer" were published in *Pirene's Fountain*

"On the Kill Line", "First in Her Family" and "Freedom of the Press" were published in *Conclave*

"Through the Plexiglass, Dimly" and "I Don't Want You to Get Shooted" were published in *Genre: Urban Arts*

"Don't Kidnap My Mom Before My First Communion" and "A Salvadoran Story" were published in the anthology *Veils, Halos and Shackles: International*

Poetry on the Abuse and Oppression of Women

"The Blessed Breeze a Day After 95 Degrees" won 1st Place in the *2022 Mississippi Valley Poets and Writers Award of the League of Minnesota Poets*

"Washing Away" was published in the anthology *The Kindness of Strangers*

"My Daughter Is" was published in *The Avenue*

"How to Write a Suicide Sermon" was published in *Poet's Choice*

"The Robin Builds Her Corona Nest" was published in *Thema*

"The Swallows Return to East 28th Street" was published in the Anthology *Goodness*

"Our Neighbor Walks His Son to the Bus Stop" was published in *Borderlands*

"The Alley That God Walks Down" was published in *Catchwater*

"Bath Time for the Robins, St. Luke's Day, October 18" was published in the *Crossings Art Center Poet-Artist Collaboration Series*

"Dying Back" and "First Snowfall on 18th Avenue" were published in *The Bacopa Literary Review*

A version of "After a November Windstorm" was published in *Arkana*

"Love Poem" was published in the anthology *Surprised by Joy*

"Emergency" was published in *Iris Literary Journal*

"Bird Spirit Man God" was published in *The Closed Eye Open*

"I Will Watch You Through the Middle of the Night" was published in *Alalitcom*, the on-line journal of the *Alabama Writer's Conclave*

"Finding Home" was published in *Carbon Culture Review*

"Breathe We Must" was published in *The Family Room*

"The Robin Builds Her Corona Nest", "The Swallows Return to East 28th Street", "Bath Time for the Robins, St. Luke's Day, October 18", "Bird Spirit Man God" and "Revenge of the Pseudo-Ravens, 2021" were published in the anthology *Petit à Petit, L'Oiseau Fait Son Nid (Little by Little, The Bird Builds His Nest)*

Patrick Cabello Hansel is a multi-genre artist and teacher who has worked in photography, drama, mosaic and creative writing. In addition to *Breathing in Minneapolis*, he is the author of the poetry collections *The Devouring Land* (Main Street Rag Publishing) and *Quitting Time* (Atmosphere Press). Nominated three times for a Pushcart Prize, he has won awards from the Loft Literary Center and MN State Arts Board.

Patrick's poems and prose have been published in over 85 journals in the U.S., England, Israel, Ireland and The Philippines. He has taught creative writing, mosaics and photography in elementary and high schools, with seniors, unhoused individuals and 1st generation immigrants. His novella *Searching* was serialized in 33 issues of *The Alley News*, a monthly newspaper in Minneapolis, and he is currently serializing its sequel *Returning*.

During his nearly 40 years of service as a Lutheran pastor in inner city churches in the south Bronx, Philadelphia and Minneapolis, he developed strategies and programs that utilized the arts for personal and community transformation. He was the founding executive director of non-profits in each of the three communities, where thousands of people learned and created murals, dramas, photography shows, cultural processions and other art forms.

In retirement, he continues to be involved in the arts and community revitalization. He is the editor of *The Phoenix of Phillips*, a literary journal by and for the most diverse community in Minneapolis. He is working on a novel set in the 1910's as well as continuing to write poems and essays. He lives in Minneapolis with his wife Luisa, and enjoys gardening, travel and spending time with his daughters and granddaughter.

Of this collection, Patrick writes: "Most of these poems were written during one of the most difficult times for Minneapolis and the neighborhood I live and work in. We were battered by COVID, by the murder of George Floyd, the ensuing destruction of so much of the community, the threats against immigrants and the democratic process. Yet in that struggle, the breath of people and of the earth continued to sustain us. These poems reflect that power."

Patrick is available for readings, workshops and classes. His website is: www.artecabellohansel.com

www.ingramcontent.com/pod-product-compliance
Lightning Source LLC
Chambersburg PA
CBHW020336170426
43200CB00006B/401